Yo Ma

Poems to my mom.

Ellen Brown

BookLeaf
Publishing

India | USA | UK

Copyright © Ellen Brown

All Rights Reserved.

This book has been self-published with all reasonable efforts taken to make the material error-free by the author. No part of this book shall be used, reproduced in any manner whatsoever without written permission from the author, except in the case of brief quotations embodied in critical articles and reviews.

The Author of this book is solely responsible and liable for its content including but not limited to the views, representations, descriptions, statements, information, opinions, and references ["Content"]. The Content of this book shall not constitute or be construed or deemed to reflect the opinion or expression of the Publisher or Editor. Neither the Publisher nor Editor endorse or approve the Content of this book or guarantee the reliability, accuracy, or completeness of the Content published herein and do not make any representations or warranties of any kind, express or implied, including but not limited to the implied warranties of merchantability, fitness for a particular purpose.

The Publisher and Editor shall not be liable whatsoever...

Made with ❤ on the BookLeaf Publishing Platform

www.bookleafpub.in

www.bookleafpub.com

Dedication

These Poems are to my mom Jeanette Lilian Walters. Who went to her mansion in the sky 10/24/23. She was a daughter, a sister, a friend, a Veteran, a caring and hard working woman, but most of all a mother. She left behind friends, family and 8 kids. However she went to meet friends, family and 5 kids. She will forever be loved and missed.

Preface

Honestly I just can't think of a better way to celebrate my mom. She was an amazing writer and I know she would be so proud to see me complete this book. So it drives me to keep going, growing and expressing my raw emotions. I also hope this helps others who have experienced such a great loss get through the pain. It's not easy but with God we will make it through.

P.S You won't see perfect grammar or spelling, but the poems are from the heart. There will be some joy but they may trigger sadness as well. More than anything I hope they help you heal and turn to God.

Acknowledgements

Thank you to my siblings and Friends who stuck with
me through thick and Thin.
Thank you to my Mom who helped me form the women
within.
Thank you to my counselor and Friend Lakeeya who's
helping me heal.
Reminding me to always be myself, and it's ok to feel.

Poem 1

Mom I miss you everyday
Tomorrow
Last week
But most of all
Today

Poem 2

The pain I feel is like no other
I thought it'd be different not having a mother
I didn't have a dad , And that wasn't so bad
But not having you, mad me angry, felt loss, and just sad

Poem 3

My first death was at age 5, it was aunt Clara, she was
the size of the bed
So when she passed away, she looked alive, when they
told me she was dead
My next death was at 7, my 4 little siblings. I didn't
realize the loss at the time
but I think it's because I was young, and you were the
only thing on ma mind
My next death I was like 10/11, my sister Rhonda and
father Joe
I put their passing together, cuz I didn't expect either one
of them to go
I don't recall any In-between, maybe there was, I don't
really Know
I just no I had to keep movin, had to stay alive, I couldn't
slow
Then I loss my 2nd mom, I was like 24 or 25
Watching her go really hurt, I still wish she was alive
And With all that death, you would think I'd be ready for
you

But I wasn't and I'm not, and I'm still trying to make do

Poem 4

Hey mom it's 11:15pm and I just got two teeth removed.
Where are you to say suck it up! You've been through
worse, God got chu!
But fr I wish you was here, this life is not the same.
I look at things different, this a new kind of pain.
A new kind of Hurt, Anger, even Joy not the same.
But I know mom, God got me; Through the sun and the
rain.

Poem 5

I had a dream about you, and it gave me peace
I was so angry and didn't know, but it gave me relief
You said you had to be with your kids, they needed you
too
I forgot everything you survived, and all that you've
been threw
I realized it was your time, and you seen more then most
You conquered a lot, so when talking about you I boast
I know you can hear me, and understand what I say
So thank you for stoping by and letting me know your
ok

Poem 6

Mom you taught us in the womb that the system would
attack
So we was always prepared, paid attention, then ready to
react
You taught me about God, before I knew what I was
Learning
You taught me how to get money, before I knew what I
was earning
I can't stress how much I miss reaching out to you
Good or bad, when you could you came through
You weren't always nice, but you tried your best
And that's what I'll remember, nothing more nothing
less

Poem 7

Yo ma I Just wanted to Thank you:
For teaching me first about Gods love thank you
For teaching me when needing help look above thank
you
You showed me how to stay strong thank you
Through hard times you help me move along thank you
For telling me I can do anything thank you
For always telling me I could sing thank you
For teaching me to watch out and duck thank you
For showing me it was God and not luck thank you

Psalm 139:13-14KJV
For thou hast possessed my reins: Thou hast covered me
in my mother's womb. I will praise thee; for I am
fearfully and wonderfully made: Marvellous are thy
works; And that my soul knoweth right well.

Poem 8

Some days without you are better then others
But today I'm just thankful you gave me my brothers
They protect me, keep me humble, & show me love all at
once
I can't imagine if you didn't have so many sons
And looking back I think God that they helped me stay
prude
I mean it wasn't just them, you helped me be rude
Don't get me wrong I gave respect, and could adjust like
water
But had no problem letting people know, I was still my
mother's daughter

Poem 9

I'm sitting in the car crying thinking about you
How it must feel to have your health and mind slowly go
To watch you not move but instead, sit and stew
To be like my little sister and watch you decline not
grow
I'm glad you pushed me away till the end, you knew me
well
You knew I couldn't bear that pain, on earth while In
hell
I guess you figured we been threw enough, and we did
no lie
You brought me in just in time, so I could watch you fly
It was surprisingly peaceful, knowing your no longer in
pain
Knowing you could stop fighting for us & fighting to
remain sane
It still hurts knowing you won't call me again "after
going threw the other Eleven"
But it's all worth it knowing your at peace,
Finally in heaven

Poem 10

I don't know if I truly thanked you, for apologizing when
I came back home
I thank God you made them keep me and my brothers
together, so I was never alone
It was crazy cuz I never thought they would keep us, we
always came back
But the Foster Care Independence Act of "99 changed
that
They said we needed permanent placement, no more
back and forth
I don't know if it was good or bad, I just know it
changed our course
And they wouldn't let us keep our last name, that part
really sucked
And they said I could only keep one middle, by then I
just felt stuck
You know me and Xavier was gonna run away we even
packed a bag
But we couldn't leave Rob and couldn't find you, so we
had to turn back

Ok now I'm rambling and I just wanted to say thank you
And like Tupac said in Dear Mama "I will always
appreciate you"

Poem 11

Another day with out you, its weird I don't like it
The tears come whenever they want no matter how ard I
fight it
My consular says let em flow, it's all apart of healing
But sometimes I be on the move and can't afford the
feeling
Then I feel bad I can't cry for you, and decide to let it
show
But then I can't stop, once I start; see here I go
It has slowed down since last year and I thank God for
that
My pops keeps me busy, I'm starting a business, and I
got a cat
You would like her! She'd fit right in with your twelve
Ma bros say don't become the next cat lady, but I'm
thinking about it what the hell

Poem 12

Halloween, Thanksgiving, and Christmas. They all
remind me of you.
You loved scary movies, dressing up and trick or treating
too
Thanksgiving was for family, and coming together
Eating, gathering, and giving thanks to one another
Christmas was the main one, the birth of Jesus and
thanking God
The smell of pine trees, having gifts or no gifts, didn't
matter it wasn't odd
You just wanted us to be together on these 3 holidays
To love of one another and give the most high praise

Poem 13

I still end the night with the Lord's Prayer
You taught it to me, so now I can share

"Our Father, who art in heaven, hallowed be thy name;
thy kingdom come; thy will be done on earth as it is in
heaven. Give us this day our daily bread, and forgive us
our trespasses, as we forgive those who trespass against
us, and lead us not into temptation, but deliver us from
evil. For God you are the Kingdom and the power and
the glory forever and ever Amen"

Another one you taught me that never gets old
This I also pray at night with out being told

Now I lay me down to sleep,
I pray the Lord my soul to keep.
If I should die before I wake,
I pray the Lord my soul to take.
God bless my mom, my dad, my siblings and
God bless me Amen.

Poem 14

I was so proud when I came by the house, and your
neighbors knew who I was
To find out you where so proud of your oldest daughter
made me blush
When I saw our pictures on the wall, I knew it was true
You where as proud of me, as I was of you
Now we where two strong women, still argued, and
sometimes you disowned me
But we both knew it was all talk. Blood in blood out at
least that's what you told me.

Poem 15

Thank you mom for always making me feel it's ok to be
crazy
To feel ok laughing out loud, working hard, but never
lazy
To be a little different, unique, outspoken and always
brave
Being high off life, saying never follow, find my own
wave
Saying never give up, no matter what, or how hard it
seemed
Even if it wasn't possible for them, it's possible for me!

Poem 16

I always knew to work hard, and that was because of
you
No matter what the job, I knew to do what I had to do
Whether I was pushing carts in-front of the grocery
store
Cutting lunch meat, flippin burgers, or cleaning floors
In all this I learned one job wasn't better then another
As long as you worked smart, you could always get
further
Work willingly in whatever ye do, see it all for the Lord
For the money is not your true pay, heavens the ultimate
reward

Poem 17

Mom the things I learned from you, I will use forever
To Hope for better always, and feel helpless never
To treat others the way I want to be treated, even when
it's hard
To give it to God over humans, cause only Thee holds the
cards
To know I will never be perfect, I can only try my best
The Bible's the book to study, and life will be the test
To thank God for giving his Son, cause forgiveness I will
need
To give and to get it, and When God speaks, take heed

Poem 18

Some times I wish pops understood, the sacrifices I made
Taking care of him while I was losing you, running back
and forth some days
Him forgetting I lost my mom, not knowing why I'm
upset
Thinking it was all about him, not seeing the deeper
regret
Now Knowing eventually he will leave me to, and then
I'm back to being alone
Back to square one figuring it all out, cuz the purpose I
had is gone
I know God, there's more to ma story, it's just hard to
see ahead some days
I know mom stop worrying & give it all to God, just get
down on my knees and pray

Poem 19

The trees are turning from green to brown, the time just
changed too
I know it seems like I'm saying anything, but it all
reminds me of you
But also green was your favorite color, and nature is
where you grew
The smell of grass, pine trees, the fog and even the
morning Dew
It all made your eyes light up, like a little kid; you where
brand new
Possibilities, ideas, the urge to clean, it all came rushing
threw
You became the Jeanette you knew you where, and
always wanted to be
No longer a rug, the glass they saw threw, Just Gods
child & truly happy

Poem 20

I don't know what the future holds, but I know I'll still
feel the loss
Of losing a queen, a love, a child of God, a independent
rebel, a boss
A genius honestly, but could play dumb whenever she
really needed
Knowing the world could not always see who you were,
or didn't believe it
But we knew as your kids, yeah we saw you clear as day
Kind at heart, and tried your best, and let no one get in
your way

Poem 21

Mom I miss you ever day, but today a little less
The pain hurts all the same, but time helps
I guess
A year seems like no time at all, but with God I'm
starting to feel
Although it can get gloomy, with The Lord
I know I will heal

www.ingramcontent.com/pod-product-compliance
Lightning Source LLC
LaVergne TN
LVHW010851200726
843508LV00012B/2863